A National Trust Series for Children

Honest Rogues

THE INSIDE STORY OF SMUGGLING

Harry T Sutton

BATSFORD – HERITAGE BOOKS

Research: R J Sutton

Design and art direction: Fetherstonhaugh Associates, London

Illustrations: Chapter 1, Ken Kirkland and Ron Stenberg; Chapters 2 and 3, John Gardner, Valerie Headland, Jane Morgan, Dan Pearce

Produced by Heritage Books

Published jointly by B T Batsford Limited and Heritage Books

Distributed by B T Batsford Limited, 4 Fitzhardinge Street, London W1H 0AH

Printed by Robert MacLehose & Co. Ltd, Glasgow

ISBN 0 7134 1725 0

Contents

'A Smugglers Song' from the Definitive Edition of Rudyard Kipling's
Verse is by permission of the National Trust and the Macmillan Company
of London and Basingstoke.

1 Tom Potter of Polperro

'Quick about it boys,' warned John Oliver, looking anxiously out to sea. ''Tis bright as day and there's revenue men about!'

One of the smugglers pointed to the brandy tub he carried in his arms.

''Tis a rare cold night, skipper,' he said. 'A drop o' this u'd make warmer work!'

'Not yet Tom,' Oliver told him. 'Get the load out first.'

And the smugglers aboard the *Lottery* went on with their work, carrying tubs to the landers' boats which lay alongside.

It was a bright moonlit night, the day after Christmas in the year 1798 and the *Lottery* was anchored in Cawsand Bay near Plymouth with a cargo of spirits brought from France. The *Lottery* and her crew were from Polperro, one of the most infamous haunts of smugglers along the entire Cornish coast, at a time when the contraband trade was at its height. Brandy, rum, tobacco, tea, coffee, silks and lace were all heavily taxed and if goods could be landed without duty being paid, there were very big profits to be made. The fishermen of Cornwall knew every cove and inlet on the coast where smuggled goods could be landed out of sight and many fishing villages made far more money from smuggling than they ever could from sales of fish.

The *Lottery*, with her crew of fishermen from Polperro, was the most successful smuggling ship – and the most wanted – from Dover to Land's End, and on this cold December night as her cargo of brandy tubs was being rowed ashore in Cawsand Bay, the risks they ran were well known to Oliver and his crew. Capture by customs officers meant long prison terms and the loss of cargo as well as ship, and lying at anchor, her sails furled and with not a breath of wind to stir the surface of the sea, the *Lottery* was helpless until she could be got under way.

Knowing this, the smugglers worked in silence, carrying the tubs from the cargo hold to the landing boats alongside. From

time to time, one would stop and listen, looking keenly across the dark waters of the bay. For ten minutes they worked. Then, suddenly, there came a warning cry from the lookout in the bows.

'Hold fast men,' said Oliver. And the crew stopped work to listen, not breathing to hear the better. There came a faint 'plash' – 'plash' from seaward.

'Oars!' cried John Oliver. 'Revenue men sure enough!'

Then came another shout from the bows.

'There they are!'

And as the smugglers watched, a boat rowed by six men came steadily towards them. A seventh man, dressed in the uniform of a customs officer, was seated in the stern. As they approached the officer shouted to the *Lottery* and a chill went through the hearts of the smugglers as they heard his words:

'I'm a revenue officer!' they heard him shout. Then he stood up and the *Lottery* crew saw him unfurl the custom house flag.

Ambrose Bowden, customs officer stationed at Cawsand in Plymouth Sound, could hardly believe his luck. He looked again through his glass at the dark outline of the vessel at anchor in the bay.

'There's not a doubt about it,' he told his men. ''Tis the *Lottery*!'

'Then we've got her this time,' said one of them. 'There's

not a breath of wind and if we're quick, she'll not get away.'

Bowden was out with his boatmen to check some of the more likely inlets and bays in Plymouth Sound, for on a bright night like this there was a good chance of surprising smugglers at their illegal work. But a chance to catch the *Lottery*! That would be a splendid prize indeed!

Most of the ships used by smugglers were luggers, fast in a good breeze but slow to turn about. But the *Lottery*, like the revenue ships, was cutter rigged and so could sail on equal terms. Built in Bristol by masters of their craft, she had many times shown herself as fast as any revenue cutter afloat. Sailing close-hauled to the wind, she had often left them far behind in a chase returning from France with her laughing crew dangling a towline astern to mock the slow pursuit.

But now, seeing at last a chance to catch the *Lottery*, Ambrose Bowden urged his men on.

'Faster, faster, men!' he told them. 'A whiff of breeze and she'll be off!' And as they came within hailing distance he shouted to them, saying who he was, and unfurling the customs flag.

The reply from the *Lottery* came at once.

'Keep off or we shall fire!'

Bowden laughed.

'I've heard that before!' he told his men. And it was true that smugglers rarely shot to kill, for they were not stupid

enough to risk their lives for a cargo worth but a few hundred pounds.

'Shoot if you like!' Bowden shouted back. 'But we're coming aboard.'

Then there came shots from the *Lottery*. Puffs of gun-smoke broke along her rail and soon the water round the revenue boat showed the rings and plops of falling shot.

'They're firing wide all right,' said the officer, with a grin. And taking up his musket, he fired a shot above the heads along the ship's rail. Then he reloaded and fired again.

Suddenly one of the men in the revenue boat stopped pulling on his oar. The boat began to slew around.

'Mind what you are about!' shouted Bowden. But then the man's oar slipped from his hands and he fell from his place to the bottom of the boat.

'Glyn is shot!' shouted one of the oarsmen. And going forward, Bowden saw that Humphrey Glyn was dead, the front of his head completely shot away.

A silence fell on the moonlit waters as both sides saw that a tragedy had taken place. But then, taking advantage of the lull, and feeling a slight breeze ruffling the gin-still sea, John Oliver ordered the *Lottery's* anchor cable cut and within moments, her canvas filling, the cutter sailed gracefully out to the open sea.

Rowing sorrowfully back to shore with their dead comrade, the revenue men of Cawsand swore vengeance on the *Lottery* crew.

'Through hell or high water,' declared Ambrose Bowden, 'we shall see the rascals hanged!'

The magistrates at Plymouth could not agree about the death of Humphrey Glyn.

'We must clean out this nest of thieves,' declared the Chairman. 'Polperro is a disgrace to Cornwall!'

Mr Carter, the churchwarden and a lover of brandy and good Virginian tobacco, was not so sure.

'The doctor says Glyn was killed by a shot which hit right in the middle of his forehead,' he reminded the Chairman.

'If the poor fellow was rowing *towards* the *Lottery* he would have had his back to the smugglers and surely, a shot from them would have hit the *back* of his head. . . .'

'Stuff and nonsense!' replied the Chairman. 'I knew Humphrey well. The fellow was always an inquisitive fool. Probably turned in his seat to see the smugglers instead of attending to his work. . . .'

'He could hardly have turned *completely* round,' suggested another magistrate. 'Surely it *might* have been a chance shot from one of his own men? It was dark at the time and perhaps . . . ?

The Chairman snorted angrily.

'Humphrey Glyn was shot dead by the crew of the smuggler ship *Lottery*' he insisted. 'And that is manslaughter in the process of defying the law.'

So an order was made for the arrest of the *Lottery* and her entire crew. There was, moreover, only one penalty for manslaughter. Every man of the *Lottery's* crew was liable to hang for the crime.

'Order out the dragoons!' demanded the Chairman of Magistrates. 'Surround Polperro and clean out that den of ruffians once and for all!'

Polperro, a fishing village of less than a thousand souls, was well placed as a home for smugglers. Nestling below sheer cliffs, the one road to the village was steep and easily watched. Customs men could never approach without warning going quickly ahead and there was always time for the smugglers to hide, not only themselves but all the contraband goods they held in store from their last adventure to the Channel Isles or the coast of France. Almost every cottage had its hidey-hole. Secret chambers, some cut into the thicknesses of walls; others simply bricked-up cellars or hidden places in roofs or outside sheds. At the first sign of trouble smugglers and their illegal wares could disappear without trace. The villagers went about their business, scrubbing steps, mending nets, cleaning fish, just like any other honest fisherfolk. But when the custom officers had gone, they laughed amongst themselves and told many tales of tricks they used to fool the guardians of the law.

But now, as the *Lottery* sailed back from Cawsand Bay, a threat lay over Polperro such that it had never known before.

John Oliver was the first man ashore.

'We had a brush with the revenue,' he told the waiting women on the quay. 'Seems like one of them was hurt for they sheered off.'

'Did 'ee shoot at 'em, skipper?' asked one of the women, And there was anxiety in her voice. It was a rule amongst Cornish smugglers that they should run and never shoot if they were in trouble and that was why the *Lottery* was the fastest ship on the coast.

'None of my lads fired a shot but what was wide of the revenue boat,' declared Oliver. 'Likely 'twas an accident if one of them got hurt.'

'Please God the revenue think the same,' remarked another woman.

'There'll be trouble else!'

For two days life in Polperro went on as usual. Contraband from the *Lottery* was unloaded and hidden away, for she was only half through with her work when surprised in Cawsand Bay. Another vessel with contraband of tea bought from an East Indiaman lying off Plymouth, came in at night and went silently away before dawn. Local merchants and farmers came to the village for supplies of tea and coffee; the squire's man called for his master's case of fine French brandy; the parson bought his usual plug of cheap tobacco and the inn-keeper took his usual keg of rum.

But then there came news from Truro. A force of dragoons and a team of riding officers were on their way to Polperro. And for an hour there was turmoil in the village. The *Lottery* set sail for a safe hideout in the Channel Isles manned by a volunteer crew; some of the smugglers hid in the village; others made off into the countryside, hiding in barns and hedgerows, waiting for the danger to pass. But it did not pass. Day after day there were customs officers patrolling the village. Sometimes, at dead of night, a troop of dragoons would come stealthily down the hill and surround houses where smugglers were thought to hide. Often the work of the village was stopped all day as homes were searched and vessels in the harbour ransacked for hidden men. None of the *Lottery* crew was safe.

The shooting in Cawsand Bay took place in December 1798 and by March next year things were getting desperate in the village. Not able to fish, or smuggle goods, the men of the *Lottery* were still in hiding, fearful night and day of discovery by customs officers or dragoons. At last a message was sent to Guernsey and one dark night in May, the *Lottery* sailed secretly back into Polperro harbour. A few hours later, John Oliver came out of hiding with his crew and, before dawn broke, they were off again to sea. Free at last! But seeing them off, their women asked amongst themselves – free for how long?

It was a fine warm afternoon in early May and Jem Stallard, riding officer in the customs service was enjoying his jog along the cliffs above Bolt Head. The sun shone, the birds sang and all was well with the world. 'Gid up there, lazybones!' Jem

called to his horse. And he gave him a gentle dig in the ribs to remind him that both were on duty that fine sunny day. Then, as the obedient horse broke into a slow trot, Jem Stallard glanced cheerfully out to sea.

'Great guns!' he exclaimed.

A cutter-rigged ship, close-hauled, was scudding along in a fair breeze, close inshore below the cliffs.

'That's a craft I've seen 'afore,' murmured the riding officer. And, dismounting, he pulled out his glass to get a closer look. Word had come from Plymouth that the *Lottery* had called at Polperro and left again late at night and all riding officers were told to keep a good lookout for her; she might try her old tricks again and run a load of contraband to the coast.

'It could be her!' said Jem. And he was just about to mount his horse and gallop to Salcombe with the news when another sail came into sight. It was a second cutter under full sail. Looking through his glass, Jem saw a long thin pendant flying at the masthead – the custom house flag – and he gave a shout of joy.

A stranger, strolling along the clifftop path that fine spring afternoon would have thought a madman loose on Bolt Head Down for Jem Stallard, unable to contain himself, was dancing up and down, waving his riding officer's hat aloft.

'Come on Hinde girl!' he was shouting. 'Keep after her,

keep after her!' And he almost fell over the cliff in excitement as he watched the chase begin.

John Oliver did not like the situation at all. Since leaving Polperro the *Lottery* had been to Holland for a cargo of gin and on the voyage back they had met headwinds all the way. Now, twelve hours late, they had arrived off the Cornish coast in daylight and there were more than four hours to pass before darkness made it safe to sail to Torcross in Start Bay. Knowing that every customs officer from Dover to Land's End would be on the watch, they did not dare to approach Polperro and they had chosen Torcross hoping that they could land a cargo there unseen.

'We'll sail close in,' decided Oliver, 'and wait 'til darkness falls.' And to slow their approach, the *Lottery* cruised gently towards Start Point under reefed mainsail and a single jib.

Captain Gabriel Bray, master of the revenue cutter *Hinde*, could hardly believe his eyes. It was broad daylight, three o'clock in the afternoon, yet there, sailing into Start Bay as bold as brass was a cutter which from its size and the shape of its slender hull could only be the smuggler ship *Lottery*. Crews wanted for murder did not often take such risks and Captain Bray had a moment of doubt as he scanned the cutter through his glass. But there could be no doubt. It was the

Lottery. And as he watched, he saw her suddenly turn about. Reefs were taken from her mainsail and extra sails were set. The *Lottery* turned and headed west, heeling over as the off-shore breeze filled her sails. And the chase was on.

For the rest of that day and through the night the two ships sailed westward, then south, then west again. Once the *Lottery* doubled back hoping to pass the revenue cutter in the night. But Captain Bray's lookout gave a warning in time and the *Hinde* turned eastward too. So the chase went on until at 5.00 a.m. dawn broke to reveal the two ships, five miles apart, sails flapping in a dead calm.

Captain Bray made the first move.

'Lower the longboats,' he ordered. 'We shall have to take her while she lies becalmed.' And with Hugh Pearce, the mate in command, two heavily armed longboats set off to make the arrest.

As the longboats approached, Pearce could see the *Lottery* crew manning long oars on each side in a desperate attempt to row the ship away. Then a gun was fired from the smuggling ship and the ball splashed into the sea beside the leading boat.

'Keep off!' came a voice through a speaking trumpet on the *Lottery*. 'If you approach nearer we shall sink both boats!'

There was an exchange of words. Hugh Pearce declared that they knew the cutter to be the *Lottery* even though her name was hidden by a canvas sheet. But John Oliver would not give in. He warned the boats to keep clear and fired several sighting shots. Until at last, remembering the fate of Humphrey Glyn in Cawsand Bay, the mate of the *Hinde* ordered the longboats to give up for that day. They had hardly returned to the *Hinde* and been taken aboard when a strong breeze blew up and the revenue cutter, favoured more than the *Lottery* by her position further out to sea, closed in on the smugglers and boarded her when both ships were close to the Longships light.

The *Lottery* was taken at last. John Oliver and seventeen men were arrested and a cargo of 716 casks of gin, some cases of tea and some tobacco were found on board. The men were taken to Plymouth where they were sent for trial. For their smuggling activities all the crew were sentenced to imprison-

ment. But there was still a much more serious charge for them to face. They could still all hang for the murder of Humphrey Glyn. They could still all stand trial for their very lives.

When news reached Polperro that the *Lottery* was caught, the villagers were in despair. Eighteen men, Polperro born, were caught and sure to hang. Women began to wear black, and talk at the inn of an evening was of dark things such as men speak of at death-beds and funerals. Imagine the surprise therefore when, a month later, news came that one man only was to be charged with the murder of Humphrey Glyn.

'Roger Toms has turned king's evidence. He accuses Tom Potter of firing the shot that killed Humphrey Glyn,' they were told.

'But where are they now?'

'Tom Potter has been taken to London to await trial. Roger Toms is with the revenue cutter at Fowey. They are keeping him safe until he gives evidence at Tom's trial.'

The villagers found it hard to believe.

Roger Toms was a good seaman. He lived with his wife in the village and was respected as were his father and grandfather before him. Tom Potter, the man he had named as a murderer, was another local man whose family had for many generations been fishermen – and smugglers – in Polperro. Both had been comrades in the crew of the *Lottery*. It was, indeed, hard to believe that one had turned traitor to his mate.

One evening, in the parlour of the Three Pilchards Inn, some fishermen of Polperro met to see what could be done.

'One thing for sure,' said one. 'Tom Potter be no more guilty than any other of the *Lottery* crew.'

'All of them was firing wide,' agreed another. 'Likely t'was a shot from one of their own guns that killed the revenue man.'

'Roger Toms is telling lies to save his own skin!' said a third. Then one fisherman, the elder of the village, got up to speak and the others fell silent.

'Only one man says Tom Potter fired the shot,' he said quietly. 'And that man is Roger Toms.'

He looked meaningfully about him at the silent men in the fire-lit parlour bar.

'If Roger Toms were out 'o the way, there'd be none to speak agin' him!'

'Aye,' agreed another, thoughtfully. 'There'd be no case agin' him but for Roger Toms!'

Mrs Toms was ashamed of what her husband had done. When she first heard the news she could hardly trust her own ears. Roger a toady to the revenue? An informer, condemning another to save his own life! It was a hard thing to believe and harder still to live with in the village where Tom Potter's family would never forget that her husband sent their son to his death.

She was in her kitchen, alone with her sad thoughts, when there was a knock and a group of village men came in and stood together by her door. Mrs Toms stood up, startled by her visitors, for it was late and there were not often callers after dark.

'Don't be afeard, missus,' said one of them, kindly. 'We're only come to ask a favour of 'ee.'

And Mrs Toms listened in silence as they told her of their plan. When they had finished, Mrs Toms rose and, tears running slowly down her cheeks, she nodded sadly in agreement with what they had said.

'Aye', she said quietly. 'I'll do it.'

Thus it was that next day, in the early afternoon, Mrs Toms set off from Polperro to walk to Polruan, another fishing village about six miles down the coast. As she walked along the cliff path, the surf breaking against the rocks far below, she thought of what the village men had said. The revenue cutter with her husband aboard had been seen entering Polruan the day before, to get a sick seaman to a doctor so it was said. Roger might be ashore and if he was she had to see him before the cutter sailed again.

'Pray God no harm comes to him from what I have to do,' she said silently to herself. And then, halfway down the steep road into Polruan, she saw him. Roger Toms, a pint jar in front of him, was sitting alone in front of an ale house by the quay.

He got awkwardly to his feet as she approached.

'Is that 'ee then, my dear?', he said. ''Tis a surprise. . . .'

'Aye,' said his wife. ''Tis me all right and a great job I've had getting away without the village a'knowing.'

She paused to see if he believed her.

'They be mighty wild agin' 'ee Roger. Whatever made 'ee do such a terrible thing?'

Roger Toms looked anxiously around as though he feared they might be overheard.

'Come inside, my dear,' he said. 'We can talk more easy there.'

So Roger Toms and his wife went inside the ale house parlour and talked together about village affairs and about the children who missed their father, of course, as all children will.

So the time passed and, just as it was getting dark, Mrs Toms rose as though to leave.

'Must 'ee go so soon then?' asked Roger.

'Aye, for 'tis getting late and there's the children to tend to.'

'Then I s'pose I'd better come some of the way with 'ee,' said Roger. But there was a doubt in his voice.

At this, Mrs Toms's heart beat faster and her hands shook a little, for this was just what she had been sent to do.

'Oh, thank 'ee, Roger,' she said. 'I would feel much safer!'

The path across the cliffs was well worn, otherwise Roger and his wife might have lost their way in the gathering dark. As it was, they walked easily up to Lantic Downs, Roger Toms chatting more cheerfully now, although his wife seemed quieter than he had known her before.

They had just reached the place where the path begins its slope to Polperro far below, when four men sprang from behind a bush. There was a brief struggle and then the informer, flung to the ground and firmly held, was secured with ropes and taken off, a prisoner.

'Do 'ee keep your word,' warned Mrs Toms, as with tears

in her eyes she watched her husband's hopeless struggles in his onetime comrades' grasp. 'Don't thee harm my man!'

'Aye missus,' promised one of them. 'He'll not get hurt.'

And so, like Tom Potter before him, Roger Toms disappeared in the secret way which the Cornish smugglers could arrange so well.

It was some hours before the customs officers found their key witness gone. Then they acted with ruthless speed. Even stronger forces of dragoons descended on Polperro and every house in the village and every room and cupboard in every house was searched and searched again.

But Toms was hidden in a secret cave at the bottom of a high cliff which the sea washed at high tide and which was hidden by jagged rocks when the tide was low. Weeks passed whilst Tom Potter awaited trial. But Roger Toms could not be found.

Then, many weeks later, a customs officer in the island of Guernsey heard that a man was hidden in a certain ship due to

sail that very day for America. The ship was searched and there was found – Roger Toms, still a prisoner in the hands of Polperro men who were at the very point of removing him from England for good.

The trial of Tom Potter began in London, at the Old Bailey, almost exactly two years after the fatal clash in Cawsand Bay.

'I was a seaman aboard the *Lottery* cutter on the night in question,' Roger Toms told the judge. 'We had sent off some loads of spirits and I went below. I then heard voices cry "Keep off!" and "It's a king's boat!" Then I heard firing and soon there were orders to cut the cable. The master with Potter and several others had a conversation. John Oliver said he should be very sorry if any harm had taken place by their firing. And Potter had replied that he had taken good level when he fired and was sure he saw a man drop.'

Tom Potter was hanged at Execution Dock, Wapping, on 18 December 1800. Roger Toms could not face the villagers of Polperro again and he stayed in London for the rest of his miserable life. He was given a job at Newgate prison and there he worked, forgotten by his wife and children, but his disgrace is remembered by the fishermen of Polperro to this day.

And the *Lottery*? She was far too fine a vessel to be destroyed after her capture. She became a revenue cutter and, in her turn, caught many an honest rogue at the contraband trade in those bad old days – not really so very long ago.

2 The Inside Story

FREE TRADERS

Suppose that some of your pocket money was taken back each week to pay part of the family gas bill, for electricity or towards paying the water rate. You would have less to spend on sweets. But you would not get any more gas or electricity or water for your money. Only less sweets. In other words, you would have been 'taxed'. And that is something that nobody enjoys.

The worst time of all for taxes in Britain was during the years from about 1700 to 1850 for then the government had to find money for wars. We fought wars in America, France, Holland and Spain during that time and there were warships to buy as well as horses, guns and swords. There were also soldiers and sailors to be paid for fighting. So taxes were put on everything to pay for it all and, of course, they were put most heavily of all on luxuries – the things people especially liked to buy.

A pound of tea, for example, could be bought for 10p in Holland, but it cost 50p a pound in England in 1760. Brandy was even more heavily taxed. A four gallon 'tub' could be bought for 80p in France where it was made but, by the time it reached the shops in England, the price had become £1.60 a bottle and the difference was mostly tax.

But if you wanted to buy tea or brandy without having to pay the tax, there was always somebody to whisper in your ear: 'Tea for only 30p a pound – save 20p. Everybody is buying it!'

It was against the law, but like the speed limits on our motorways, the law was difficult to enforce. There were secret coves and river mouths, quiet hidden bays and tiny fishing havens like Polperro where goods could be landed without paying tax. The customs men could not be everywhere at once. But, like the motorway police, they watched and sometimes laid traps to catch the smugglers. There were exciting chases at sea and sometimes fighting on land. When smugglers banded together to defy the law, soldiers were called in to help. Yet, all along the south coast of England from Dover to Land's End, the smugglers went about their work. Free traders they were called and most people bought smuggled goods when they could find them.

It became a game. A very dangerous game. The smugglers hid their contraband and the customs men sought it out. Brave, and cruel things, happened on both sides. Now we shall see the real Inside Story of what went on.

THE SHIPS
The smugglers usually sailed ships called 'luggers' because they had 'lug' sails which were square in shape and fixed to their masts like this:

The revenue ships were 'cutter' rigged. Their sails were more like those used on modern yachts and were fixed to the masts like this:

The hulls of the two ships were shaped differently.

Lugger

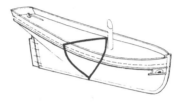

Cutter

Both the revenue and the smuggling ships were armed with swivel and carriage guns.

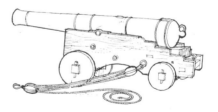

Carriage gun

The revenue cutters had to be stoutly built so that they could crash alongside a smuggler ship in a heavy sea without risk of their hull being stove in. The smugglers' ships could be built less heavily and they also had a more shallow draught so that they could sail into shallower water than the revenue cutters.

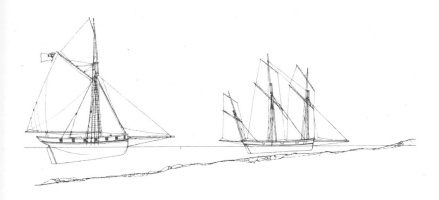

To get away from the revenue cutters which were faster than them, the smugglers of Deal in Kent invented a 'speedboat' which did not depend upon the wind at all. The 'engine' was provided by as many as twenty strong men pulling oars, and the boats, called galleys, were often seventy feet long and eighteen feet wide.

It is interesting that a Viking longship found in a burial mound in Norway was almost the same size – seventy-nine feet long by seventeen feet wide. This ship was built more than a thousand years before the smugglers' galleys – in A.D. 750. The Vikings had sixteen oars in each side of their ships whereas the smugglers had only ten. But then the Vikings were not concerned with barrels of brandy or rum, so they had more room for fighting men to row their ships.

In their galleys the smugglers of the south coast could cross to France at a steady speed of nine knots and easily make the return journey in one day. If they were chased by revenue cutters they simply turned and rowed directly into wind where the customs ships could not follow! They could row into shallow water and twenty men could easily lift their long, slender craft and carry it up a beach. On several occasions the smugglers from Deal and Dover landed deliberately on the dangerous Goodwin Sands at low tide and carried their galley

across to the other side. Then they casually rowed home, leaving the revenue cutters far behind.

These were the ships that sailed round Britain's coast in the early days of smuggling. The ships of both sides were well matched and so were their crews. Their game was played for high stakes.

THE REVENUE MEN

The customs service set up to challenge the smugglers was arranged rather like a football or hockey team. The forwards, fast running and quick to tackle their opponents, were the revenue cutters. In 1800 there were forty of these, manned by seven hundred men and armed with two hundred guns. They had a captain, a mate and a number of mariners, depending on the size of the ship. They were expected to stay at sea in all weathers, and especially at night, for darkness and rough seas were the friends of smugglers. They were paid largely on results for if they captured a smuggler at sea, the contraband was sold and the customs men took a share of the money received. The signal of the customs cutter which marked it out from a normal ship was a long thin flag called a 'pendant' flown at the masthead. Only warships and customs cutters in action were allowed to fly it (although, of course, some cunning smugglers hoisted one to put the customs off!). It was a rule that no revenue cutters could challenge a smuggler's ship without first hoisting their pendant. It identified them as Government ships – just as hockey or football teams wear coloured jerseys to show which side they are on.

The crew of the cutter must have looked very colourful for the men wore red flannel shirts and blue trousers whilst the officers, captain and mate, wore a blue frock coat with brass buttons, the buttonholes worked in silver thread, and a cocked hat with a cockade. Very much like the naval officers' uniform of the time. They wore swords and, when trouble was at hand, they carried pistols as well. There were guns for the crew as the smugglers of Polperro knew only too well. And cutlasses for fighting hand to hand.

Scattered round the south coast, watchful for suspicious

craft, at sea in all weathers, the 'forwards' of the customs team were worthy opponents for the smugglers.

But a line of forwards does not make a hockey team and the half-backs in the customs service were the riding officers. These mounted men were positioned along the coast within a few miles of each other with a chief riding officer in charge of six horsemen. Their job was to ride along the coast, looking into quiet bays and secret coves for signs of smuggling activities, and if a landing was discovered, the riding officer would gallop off to collect others and then, banded together, a number of them would surround the smugglers – unless, as so often happened, they were too late! If they saw suspicious ships at sea they warned the revenue cutters, which Jem Stallard was ready to do when he saw the *Lottery* at Land's End.

The full-backs of the customs team were in each port where ships arrived to unload their cargoes. There was the landwaiter who watched the landing of all imported goods, the coastwaiter who watched the landing of goods from other British ports, the tidesurveyor who had a boat and visited all ships as they arrived at the ports, and tidesmen who were left on each ship to watch the unloading.

And the goal-keeper? If all else failed they could call out the Army – the dragoons who surrounded Polperro – and the Navy also if force was needed at sea. And in the last resort, there was the Court of Law and the hangman's rope.

It was a strong team of professionals; one that should always have won the cup. But now it is time to look at the Inside Story of the smugglers themselves and see how they beat the law.

THE SMUGGLERS' TEAM

At sea the fast sailing luggers or cutters were the forwards of the smugglers' team. But they, also, had half-backs, backs and a goalkeeper to get their smuggled goods ashore. Behind the master of the lugger and his crew there was first of all the venturer or investor who put up the money for a smuggling trip. A loan of four or five hundred pounds to buy brandy in France could bring the investor a nice little profit – unless the ship was taken on its way home. Then there was the lander, he was one of the half-backs in the team for the contraband was passed to him at the shore line and he had tub carriers, local workmen, miners or fishermen, who carried the goods inland – and batmen, armed with staffs or 'bats' to guard them on the way. And the goalkeeper? Well, just as the customs men had the army and the law to help them in the last resort, so the smugglers had a law of their own.

As you saw in the story about Polperro, when something went wrong, the smugglers helped each other and were helped by the villagers to hide their goods and themselves, where they could not be found. The smugglers' great strength lay in the fact that ordinary people did not look upon them as criminals at all. They wanted to buy their cheap goods and, calling them 'free-traders', people were pleased when they outwitted the customs men and got their goods ashore.

Rudyard Kipling wrote a poem about it. (The 'gentlemen', of course, were the smugglers.)

If you wake at midnight, and hear a horse's feet,
Don't go drawing back the blind, or looking in the street,
Them that asks no questions isn't told a lie.
Watch the wall, my darling, while the Gentlemen go by!
    Five and twenty ponies
    Trotting through the dark –
    Brandy for the Parson,
    'Baccy for the Clerk;
    Laces for a lady, letters for a spy,
And watch the wall, my darling, while the Gentlemen go by!

Running round the woodlump if you chance to find
Little barrels, roped and tarred, all full of brandy-wine,
Don't you shout to come and look, nor use 'em for your play.
Put the brushwood back again – and they'll be gone next day!

If you see the stable-door setting open wide;
If you see a tired horse lying down inside;
If your mother mends a coat cut about and tore;
If the lining's wet and warm – don't you ask no more!

If you meet King George's men, dressed in blue and red,
You be careful what you say, and mindful what is said.
If they call you 'pretty maid,' and chuck you 'neath the chin,
Don't you tell where no one is, nor yet where no one's been!

If you do as you've been told, 'likely there's a chance,
You'll be give a dainty doll, all the way from France,
With a cap of pretty lace, and a velvet hood –
A present from the Gentlemen, along 'o being good!
    Five and twenty ponies
    Trotting through the dark –
    Brandy for the Parson,
    'Baccy for the Clerk.
Them that asks no questions isn't told a lie –
Watch the wall, my darling, while the Gentlemen go by!

A DISAPPEARING TRICK AT SEA

If they could, smugglers avoided a clash with customs men by
running away. But there was always a risk that the wind might
drop and leave them helpless (like the *Lottery* in Cawsand
Bay). Or they might be seen as they approached the coast by a
riding officer who would gallop off and set a revenue cutter
to head them off. It was important, therefore, that a customs
officer should find no contraband aboard and many disappearing
tricks were used.

One ship, for example the *Wig Box* of Folkestone, had
hollow masts, oars, bowsprit and fenders. Between them these
hollow places could be filled with six gallons of brandy or rum.
Inside most ships it was easy to build any number of secret
places, behind bulkheads, behind sliding panels in cabins and

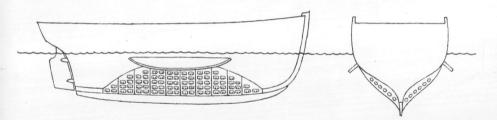

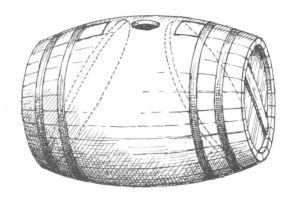

saloons, and even in false ceilings, papered over freshly for every trip. The cargo could also hide contraband. A perfectly honest cargo of cider barrels, for example, could have hidden compartments in the barrels themselves where a huge quantity of tobacco could be hidden. Crew members sometimes wore specially made bags under their normal clothes in which were hidden quantities of tea or lace to be taken ashore. The seamen must have looked very fat and well fed as they waddled ashore, and, of course, that idea was soon found out.

Smugglers were most likely to be caught when their goods were being taken ashore, and they had many tricks to keep the customs men away at this dangerous time. First, of course, they worked at night for then a ship approaching the coast was not easily seen from the shore. To guide the ships and to signal that all was safe, the landers used a special lantern with a spout so that the light was only visible out at sea. And then,

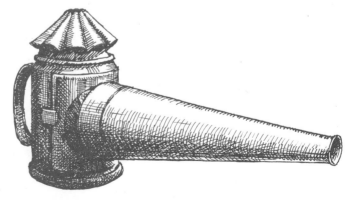

once the 'coast was clear' (a smuggling term we still use today), barrels and crates could be brought ashore and carted off to hiding places inland.

In the days of sailing ships, however, it was difficult for a vessel to approach the coast without being seen. It took too long for the whole trip to be done in darkness and there was a good chance of them being seen and the customs men alerted. If they could, therefore, the smugglers preferred to unload their contraband at sea for the landers to take ashore when the customs men were busy somewhere else. They had several ways of doing this.

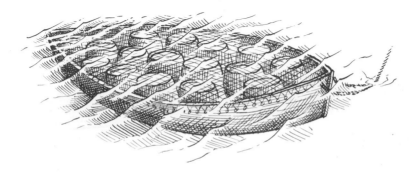

The smugglers of Selsey invented a submarine which could be filled with tubs of brandy and towed behind a ship – where it was invisible below the surface. It was a long, narrow flat-bottomed boat with a hole in the bottom to make it sink and a fishing net covering the upperside to keep the brandy tubs secure. It was towed towards the coast on an incoming tide and then released so that it drifted slowly inshore where, after dark, it could be found and its contents secured by the landers when the coast was clear of customs men.

Another trick was to tie the tubs together on a long rope and drop them overboard attached to a heavy stone. Later, the lander would row out in a small boat towing a kind of anchor. It was called a 'rock creeper' because it did not get trapped among the rocks but would catch the rope of the barrels so that they could be hauled on board.

One smuggling crew from Christchurch had the best idea of

all. On a rising tide there is a very strong current through the narrow entrance into Christchurch harbour and one of their men, a powerful swimmer, used to 'swim' a string of tubs into the bay on the flood tide at night. Many a time the customs men watched the smugglers' ship sailing slowly past the harbour entrance only to sheer off again without stopping. They did not see the splash as ten tubs of brandy and one strong swimmer slipped into the water just out of sight!

LANDERS, TUBMEN AND BATMEN

The customs man's best chance was to find smuggled goods as they were brought ashore. It was difficult and very hard work carrying heavy tubs and crates up a pebbly beach in the dark. It took time and that was the riding officers' chance. The four-gallon brandy tubs were roped together in pairs for easy carrying. The tubmen, therefore, had to carry one four-gallon tub in front and another behind with the rope over his shoulders between. The total weight of this load was about fifty kilos, which is the weight of a small motorcycle! So if he was seen by a customs man the only thing to do was drop his load and run!

For a time, that is exactly what happened. If they were seen, the landers and their tubmen made a hasty escape leaving their contraband to be collected, and later sold, by the customs men.

The story of smuggling at sea is full of adventure and excitement for this was a battle fought out between expert seamen matching sailing skills and cunning. On land it was different. As smuggling became more and more profitable, the landers with their teams grew bolder. Before long they had formed gangs, often hundreds strong, and they marched inland with their loads of contraband, quite openly and in daylight, defying the customs men and even the dragoons when they were called out to help. There were pitched battles and many were killed on both sides.

The most famous of the smuggling gangs came from Hawkhurst, a village in Kent about fifteen miles inland from the coast at Hastings. They became so successful that, not content with the profits from contraband, they turned to highway robbery and even raided inns or farmhouses demanding money and valuables, not hesitating to kill anybody who dared to stand in their way.

On one occasion, twenty of the Hawkhurst gang marched into the Mermaid Inn at Rye in Sussex and in a short time drank themselves into a state of wild drunkenness. Late that evening, singing and shouting, they staggered out of the inn, firing off their pistols just like cowboys in a Wild West film. As they came out they noticed a young local man named James Marshall, who was watching them curiously. Too curiously they must have thought, for in true Wild West style, they carried him off with them – and poor James was never seen again.

An even more 'Western' scene took place close to Hawkhurst where most of the gangsters lived. The villagers of Goudhurst, a few miles away, detested their brutal neighbours. No Goudhurst home was safe from the gang who, passing through the village, might stop at any time and break into a house to demand all the money, food and valuables they possessed. It was not safe to drink at night at the inn, nor go to church on Sundays for fear of the Hawkhurst gang.

At last, in the year 1747, a young Goudhurst man named George Sturt came home from the war to find his native village in a state of absolute terror. The people had become so afraid that they were planning to leave the village altogether and start up somewhere else where they would be safe. George Sturt, a trained soldier, persuaded the villagers not to give up but to fight back. He formed the 'Goudhurst Band of Militia' and declared that if the Hawkhurst gang dared to rob the village again, they would be opposed by force.

When Thomas Kingsmill, the Hawkhurst leader, heard of the villagers' plan he sent an immediate challenge.

'On April 20,' he declared, 'the Hawkhurst men will march into Goudhurst, murder everybody in it and then raze it to the ground!'

George Sturt, now nicknamed the 'General', was not at all afraid. He prepared Goudhurst for the great day. Trenches were dug, posts for snipers were prepared high up in trees, on rooftops, in attics and on top of the church tower. Every musket that could be found was cleaned and made ready. The women helped to make bullets with lead stripped from the church roof. And everybody was trained by George Sturt in exactly what they had to do.

Thomas Kingsmill expected that the very name 'Hawkhurst Gang' would cause the villagers to give in. So instead of making a careful approach to Goudhurst on April 20, he led his men straight into the village, firing muskets and pistols into the windows of houses as they went. Imagine their surprise – and horror – when suddenly they found themselves in the middle of return fire which seemed to be coming from every direction at once! They had fallen into an ambush in true 'Western' style.

Kingsmill's brother was the first to fall. The gang made an easy target as, bemused by the surprise of the attack, they tried to return the fire. Soon two other men lay dead, and the rest of the gang gave up and ran, chased by the cheering villagers who killed two more as they went. They even captured some of the Hawkhurst men and handed them over to be tried and later hanged. It is said that from that day, Goudhurst had no more trouble from their badly beaten neighbours.

THE PENALTIES

When the law caught up with smugglers it made quite sure that everybody should know how serious was their crime. Along with pirates and highwaymen, their special punishment was to be executed by hanging and then to hang from a gibbet in chains.

It was a very grisly punishment for the chains were used to keep the corpse from falling apart as it began to rot away. The preparations were too awful for some men to bear. Whilst the condemned man was in his cell, awaiting execution, a blacksmith came to measure him for his chains, and this upset one smuggler so badly that he died from a heart attack brought on by fright. The execution was, of course, in public and became a holiday spectacle to which people flocked as we would to a circus or a fair. Often more than one smuggler was executed at a hanging and then a row of gallows was built, placed close together so that a long farm wagon could be used as a platform on which the condemned men would stand.

Rope halters were fixed to the gallows and tied around the men's necks in a slip-knot. Then the cart was driven away leaving the poor wretches to swing until they strangled to death; a dreadful end, for they sometimes took as long as five minutes to die.

The final act was even more ghastly for the corpses were taken down and then dipped into tar to make them waterproof.

Chains and metal links were then fitted to bodies and limbs and the grim remains were hung from a strong wooden frame – the gibbet – which was usually placed in some public place near the scene of the crime.

THE TRUTH ABOUT SMUGGLERS

What then was the truth? Were smugglers just ordinary, honest rogues, supplying a demand for cheap goods? Were they only taking advantage of a bad law which could not be enforced – like modern motorists on a motorway when the speed cops are not around? The truth is that there was a Tom Potter, a quiet fisherman who was only getting 'Brandy for Parson' and 'Baccy for the Clerk' and was almost certainly hung for a crime he did not commit. And then there were bullies like Thomas Kingsmill who deserved the punishment he got. In between, it is difficult to blame the smugglers when respectable men like magistrates, doctors, even the local squire and their wives too, were their eager customers.

They were bad taxes which the customs men could not enforce and when at last they were lifted, smuggling ended because it had ceased to pay. Or, almost ended. For the customs men at our modern airports and seaports are as busy as ever. But now they are looking for drugs, precious stones, illegal currency and gold. The riding officers still watch the coasts but they are coastguards now and mostly ride in cars. Only the methods have changed – and we shall have the customs men on our tracks if we start to tell the Inside Story of that!

3 See Where It Happened

Smugglers needed secret places around the coast where they could land their contraband. They needed hiding places too, for themselves and their illegal goods. Many of the seaside places they used are now holiday towns with promenades and piers so that no traces are left of their exciting smuggling days.

Some old pubs used by smugglers have survived even in modern towns and there are many churches and cottages which could tell a tale or two. There is a list of some of these on pages 45–6.

But some of the best places to see where smugglers carried on their secret trade are now in the care of the National Trust, which preserves these places for us and future generations to enjoy and wonder at. Here now is a list of places looked after by the National Trust which were once the 'playing fields' of smugglers and revenue men all those years ago.

CORNWALL
Boscastle
Many of the coves along the North Cornish coast were used by smugglers. On the cliff above the harbour at Boscastle you can still see a square, white look-out tower built by the customs men to keep watch on the smugglers.
Dodman Point
Right on the top of the headland you can see a lonely hut. This was once a watch-house for the revenue men. It was probably built about the time the *Lottery* made trips in this area.
Morwenstow
Here you can see the rectory and church served by the Rev. Steven Hawker in the nineteenth century. He was a local character and knew many of the smugglers who lived around his parish. He used to tell the children of the parish stories of famous smugglers in the area. The most daring was Cruel

Coppinger who led a gang of smugglers in his ship the Black Prince along the Cornish coast for many years.

Mullion Cove

This is a fine natural harbour which was used by smugglers to land their goods. There are also several smugglers' caves here which can be visited.

Polperro and Polruan

This is where the *Lottery* came from. Most of the walk along the coast between Polperro and Polruan where Mrs Toms went to see her husband is now owned by the National Trust.

Talland

Robert Mark, who was one of the *Lottery's* crew when she was captured by the Hinde in 1799, is buried in Talland churchyard. You can see his epitaph there. He was shot in 1802 while at the helm of a smuggling boat trying to escape from a customs cutter. Talland churchyard was used by smugglers to store their contraband after unloading it on the beach below.

Path from Polperro

The National Trust owns Talland cliff nearby. You can get a good view of the village and the church from there.

Whitesand Bay

About three miles north of Rame Head there is an area of National Trust land that looks over Whitesand Bay. Many exciting encounters between smuggling boats and revenue cutters took place in this bay. Nearby, although it is not owned by the National Trust, is Cawsand Bay where the *Lottery's* great adventure began.

CUMBRIA

Borrowdale

There was a lot of smuggling in the Lake District. Today you can follow the routes the smugglers took inland from White-haven, Ravenglass and Seascale on the coast. One route went to Borrowdale through Wasdale Head and Sty Head Pass. The other went through Hardknott Pass and Wrynose Pass to Langdale.

DEVON

Branscombe and Beer Head

This is the site of many of Jack Rattenbury's exploits. He was a famous smuggler in this part of Devon. He wrote about his adventures in a book called *Memoirs of a Smuggler*. There are many caves in the cliffs here that were used by smugglers like Jack and his men.

Lundy Island

Thomas Benson, who was M.P. for Barnstaple, bought Lundy in 1755. All the time he pretended to be an honest M.P. he was really using Lundy as a centre for smuggling goods into the Bristol Channel area. Today the island is most famous for its puffins, but you can still see the cave under the ruins of Marisco Castle where Benson stored his contraband, and a smuggler's path which winds up the side of the cliffs.

DORSET

Brownsea Island

Because it is at the entrance to Poole Harbour, Brownsea Island must have seen many smuggling and revenue boats passing by. It was probably used by some smugglers as a hiding place too.

Whitenothe Cliff

The path which goes round the cliff was once used by smugglers as an escape route. It is mentioned in the exciting smuggling tale 'Moonfleet' by J. W. Falkner.

WEST SUSSEX

Highdown Hill

On the top of the hill, next to the National Trust land, you can still see a lonely tomb which was built by a miller called John Oliver in 1766. The story is that he used the tomb to store contraband in. When he died in 1793 the brandy had to make way for him!

EAST SUSSEX

Alfriston

This little village was a notorious smuggling place. There are two pubs here associated with a local smuggler called Stanton Collins. They are The Smugglers Inn and the Star Inn. The National Trust owns the old Clergy House in Alfriston. In Stanton Collins's time it was used as labourers' dwellings. Who knows, some of the 'labourers' might have been smugglers!

ISLE OF WIGHT

Mottistone

In the churchyard there is a tomb with a large slab of stone as a lid. At one time it was used by the local smugglers to store their contraband. Nearby the church you can see the Smuggler's Lane along which they carried their goods up from the shore.

NORFOLK

Horsey Mill

The mill you can see today is built on the foundations of an earlier one which was used by Norfolk smugglers. They used it to store goods they had brought up from the coast. If there was danger from the customs men at Yarmouth the smugglers' friends there used to send a warning by 'windmill telegraph'. Each windmill between Yarmouth and Horsey fixed its sails upright. The message could reach Horsey in fifteen minutes!

NORTH YORKSHIRE

Ravenscar

The beaches were a favourite landing place for local smugglers.

Today you can see one of the small signalling chambers they used to let the boats know when the coast was clear. It is cut into a slab of rock at the bottom of the Raven Hall Hotel gardens. When a lantern was put in the chamber it could only be seen from the sea. You can see it from the National Trust land below the gardens.

Now here are some other places where you can see things connected with smugglers.

CHURCHES AND TOMBSTONES
Old Hunstanton, Norfolk
In the churchyard you can see the gravestone of a dragoon called William Webb. He was killed by smugglers in 1784.
Binstead, Isle of Wight
Look for the gravestone of Thomas Sivell in the churchyard. He was shot by customs officers when he was sixty-four.
Kinson, Dorset
This church was used by smugglers for storing goods brought ashore at Branksome Chine. They hid them in the belfry. In the churchyard you can see the grave of Robert Trotman, a smuggler.
Patcham, West Sussex
Daniel Scales was a smuggler in this area. He was shot by revenue officers in 1796. His tombstone is in the churchyard.
Wyke, Dorset
Look for a gravestone with a carving of two ships on it. One is a lugger, the other is a revenue cutter called the *Pigmy*. This is the grave of William Lewis who was killed during the chase between the two ships.

PUBS AND OTHER PLACES
Baxtergate, near Whitby, North Yorkshire
Outside the 'Smuggler's Cafe' there is wooden figurehead. It was taken from a smuggling boat which had been sawn into pieces by customs men. The cafe was originally a pub used by smugglers.

Blackgang Chine, Isle of Wight
You can see various things associated with smugglers here, including a smugglers' cave.

Bucklers Hard, Hampshire
This little place was once a smuggling centre. The cobbler's house, which is now the chapel, had a cellar for storing contraband. The cobbler obviously did more than repair shoes!

Budleigh Salterton, Devon
The Fairlynch Arts Centre and Museum used to be a smuggling den. You can still see the cellar where goods were kept and you can climb into the lookout-tower where the smugglers kept watch for revenue men.

Goudhurst, Kent
The church tower where the villagers fought against the Hawkhurst gang is still there.

Rye, East Sussex
The Hawkhurst gang used to plan their trips in the Mermaid Inn. It is called the Mermaid Hotel now – some secret rooms and passages have been found there. In Church Square is the 'house with the crooked chimney'. It used to be the custom house.

Hastings, East Sussex
St Clement's Caves under West Hill are supposed to have been used by smugglers.

Poole, Dorset
This is where the Hawkhurst gang broke into the custom house. The one you can see today was built a little later in 1813, but it gives a good idea of what they were like.

Saltburn, Cleveland
John Andrew was a famous smuggler on this coast. He owned the Ship Inn and the White House nearby. He had a fast cutter called the *Morgan Rattler*. He hid his contraband under the floor of the stables at the White House.

MUSEUMS
Ventnor, Isle of Wight
Museum of the History of Smuggling, Undercliffe Drive. This has the biggest collection on smuggling in the country.

The Mermaid Inn, Rye

Polperro, Cornwall
Museum of Smuggling, Talland Street.
Small but interesting collection.

Hastings, East Sussex
Fisherman's Museum, Rock a Nore Road.
You can see a fishing lugger here. It is very like some of the smaller boats used by smugglers.

Poole, Dorset
Maritime Museum, Poole Quay, Paradise Street.
This is a new museum which includes a special smuggling display.

Rye, East Sussex
Rye Museum. This museum contains a few exhibits to do with smugglers and smuggling.

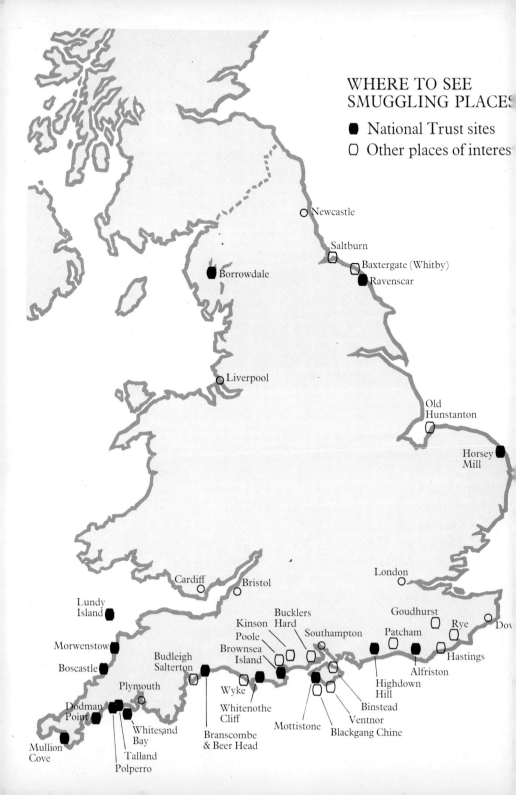

WHERE TO SEE SMUGGLING PLACES

- ⬛ National Trust sites
- ⬜ Other places of interest

Newcastle

Saltburn

Baxtergate (Whitby)

Borrowdale

Ravenscar

Liverpool

Old Hunstanton

Horsey Mill

London

Cardiff

Bristol

Lundy Island

Goudhurst

Kinson

Bucklers Hard

Rye

Poole

Southampton

Patcham

Dov

Morwenstow

Brownsea Island

Budleigh Salterton

Hastings

Boscastle

Highdown Hill

Alfriston

Plymouth

Wyke

Binstead

Dodman Point

Whitenothe Cliff

Ventnor

Whitesand Bay

Mottistone

Blackgang Chine

Mullion Cove

Branscombe & Beer Head

Talland

Polperro